# It Only Gets Worse From Here

Zachary “Noodle” Newell

Photo by: J.Mathewson Photography
Photo Illustrations by: Karissa Stivers

ISBN: 978-81-8253-896-2

First Edition: 2022
Rs. 200/-

Cyberwit.net
HIG 45 Kaushambi Kunj, Kalindipuram
Allahabad - 211011 (U.P.) India
http://www.cyberwit.net
Tel: +(91) 9415091004
E-mail: info@cyberwit.net



Printed at Thomson Press India Limited.

This book was about accomplishing something I never did before. Through struggles brought on by myself and others, I wanted to express my feelings and help not only myself, but others through the art of poetry. After everything I have been through so far in life, I found it is important to never take things too seriously. Learn to love through the bad times. Learn to stay humble during the great times. Learn to laugh all the time. After all, you just purchased a book written by a police officer named, "Noodle"

# Contents

# Chapter 1. Finding Love

## My Wolf to Your Moon

My Wolf is strong and mighty
When it's running in its pack.
Pride is overflowing,
Everything intact.

Your Moon is bright and glowing,
Illuminating all it sees.
Beauty is everlasting,
Bringing mountains to their knees.

My Wolf found itself alone.
The pack full astray.
Losing sight of everything good.
All the love had gone away.

Your Moon found my Wolf.
Lost, wandering in the dark.
It smiled and shined as it does,
Knowing what next to embark.

My Wolf felt the warmth,
From Your Moon's embrace.
It longed to feel the rays,
On his fur and on his face.

Your Moon held My Wolf,
Long throughout the night.
Love filled My Wolf.
Your Moon absorbing all his sight.

My Wolf knew Your Moon had to go.
But knew it would return again.
My Wolf longed for the night.
To the sky he would ascend.

Your Moon loved My Wolf.
Seeing him was never too soon.
My Wolf forever longed for the night,
My Wolf loved Your Moon.

## Road Trip

Whether it's driving for food,
Or picking up a new nightstand.
As long as you are in shotgun,
I'd take these tires over any land.

Removing my eyes from the road
Only to catch your gaze.
Watching your hair in the wind
Causes my heart rate to raise.

Resting my hand on yours.
Belting any song on the radio.
I'd take any trip to and from
If you are with me when I go.

I will always keep the tank full.
I will ensure the tires never slip.
Just promise you will always join me
On life's every Road Trip.

# She is Beauty

She sleeps all day
Just to fight at night.
She masks pain and anger
With compassion and love.

Music is her outlet.
The sadder the better.
But when the time comes,
She is nothing but a smile

Her calmness is like a cool breeze.
Her ferocity like a volcano.
And when it's all over
She will be seen as a sunrise.

For the good and the bad
Cannot unbalance what is.
Through all she is.
She is beauty.

# As I Dream

A mother's hug,
A moonlight's beam.
It's a warm embrace.
As I Dream.

I see your eyes.
I feel your touch.
I've never wished,
To sleep so much.

My heart's content.
My worries flee.
As the dream theater plays,
It's just you and me.

A mini vacation.
Paradise in bed.
And I have all the memories
Stored inside my head.

When my day is bad.
When you aren't near.
I crawl into bed.
And happiness will appear.

Being with you is bliss.
We are my favorite team.
Having you, day and night,
But importantly, As I Dream.

# First Date

Just like a child,
At their first dance.
Your hands feel clammy.
Your heart beating out of your chest.

Trying to think of anything to say,
Just to hear their voice respond.
Trying your best not to stare.
Wanting this date to never end.

Wishing only for this to be
The first night of many.
Praying, hoping, and begging.
Could this be the new forever?

# How I know It's You

Your smile lifts my spirit.
Your body burns my soul.
Your touch drives me crazy.
Your kiss makes me whole.

I dream of your beauty.
I desire nothing but your time.
To hold you in my arms,
Makes the world feel it's mine.

So, if you have any doubt
Or just thought it's not pure.
I will reassure you my intentions,
And reiterate so you feel sure.

There are infinite reasons,
But these are just a few.
They are the things to let me know,
How I know it's you.

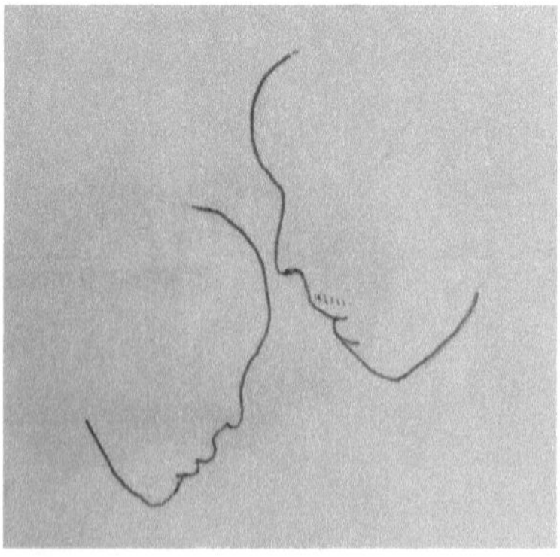

# Those Green Eyes

Like the Greek myth of Medusa,
That gaze turns men to stone.
The heart skips a beat.
The unsure becomes known.

Uncertainties become clear,
As those eyes touch the soul.
The lame able to walk.
The broken now whole.

Seconds feel like years,
Never wanting to look away.
Willing to face any evil,
As long as those moons stay.

They are immersed with magic.
Able to see through any disguise.
Leaving everyone left wanting
The sight of Those Green Eyes.

# Soul Flame.

Like a candle on the window,
Your flame dances slowly on its own.
A small light in the darkness
The only warmth you ever known.

And one day you find another fire.
Attracted to it like a moth to a light.
You yearn to feel it's warmth.
You want to harness its fight.

Finally, the two flames collide,
And the inferno leaves you in awe.
Nervous and excitement overtake.
A thing of beauty, holding no flaw.

As years past those flames only grow.
Burning hotter and brighter, unable to tame.
And that is how you know love is eternal.
Living through your Soul Flame.

# Our Book.

Badly dealt hands.
No one would look.
So, we came together,
We wrote our book.

The words ran together
Like being together all along.
The meanings so deep.
There could be no wrong.

The lines and rhymes danced
Like a flickering light.
Love was embodied
From morning to night.

Meanings so clear.
Feelings couldn't be missed.
And all this work was started.
With an awkwardly placed kissed.

So when time fades,
And foundations are shook.
One thing will always remain.
The most important; Our Book.

# Cingulomania

My desire to live is met only
With my desire to hold you.
A dream I never want to awake.
My cure to all when I'm feeling blue.

Your embrace is a pandemic
And I want no cure.
Let it infect me.
Send me into that euphoric blur.

I'd pass up the chance to be king.
I'd give up every possession.
Forever wanting to hold you
Will be my everlasting profession.

# Feel My Love.

My heart though cold,
Burns like the sun.
When we lay together,
I feel as though we're one.

I can't move a mountain.
I can't drain the sea.
There are many things,
That I wish I could be.

But one thing that I'm determined,
To achieve than all the above.
Is to bring you happiness
And make you Feel My Love.

## Nothing is Better.

Seeing your smile,
Or hearing you speak.
Nothing is better.
It always makes me weak.

But if I had to compare.
Or dare to come close.
These are the things
That are like it most.

Sharpening a pencil
From a brand-new box.
Coming inside from the cold
And putting on a warm pair of socks.

Getting a good grade.
Having a parent say they're proud.
Laying in a field of grass
While staring up at a cloud.

Getting caught in the rain.
Making someone laugh.
Having a good cry.
Taking a long bath.

The comparisons are endless
And you would agree if you met her.
But at the end of it all I can say.
Nothing is Better.

# First Love.

Wanting nothing but to feel a touch.
Desire nothing but to feel enough.
But what is sought has been always there.
Easily found if you'd only dare.
This love that you ask is at your grasp.
It held you up when you would collapse.
It brought you a smile through the tears.
Kept away the darkness for all these years.
The love I speak, reflects through the mirror.
Seemingly inadequate, but it's just the fear.
Another's love was not your first.
Some say it's a blessing and others a curse.
Accept this fact and keep it above.
For you, yourself, is your first love.

## Holidays with You

Each day with you is a blessing.
Each holiday is a cheer.
And what way to start it off,
Then staying up with you on the New Year.

Next up is a day with love.
I try to relax and walk the line.
But my excitement is overwhelming.
Knowing you are my Valentine.

Then it's a day of freedom.
And from sacrifice no one can deny.
Loving you in this great country,
Celebrating the 4th of July.

Moving on is a day of candy and fear.
Witches and goblins can be seen.
But with you I am never scared.
Kissing you on Halloween.

Closing in on a day of feasts.
Hearts and stomachs full and unforgiving.
But we rest together to mend it all.
Napping with you on Thanksgiving.

Finally, a day with gifts and snow.
You are always on the top of my list.
You are the only present I need,
Waking up to you on Christmas.

# Hands of Stone

Giving him a chance was a risk.
You heard stories and had some doubt.
He was mysterious, keeping to himself.
You weren't quite sure what he was about.

Rarely spoke about his day,
His feelings were like a myth.
There weren't many things you knew,
To add to this man's short list.

But with time you solved the puzzle.
You learned what slept inside this man.
You discovered the strength of his love.
Knew he would be your biggest fan.

Though he was work driven,
You knew he'd never leave you alone.
His heart though big, was soft and warm.
As he kept his Hands of Stone.

# My Moon and Stars

From nights of walking dogs,
To random trips in the car.
I knew you were special,
Like the Moon and the Stars

Your smile is enticing,
Reaching me near and far.
A light in the darkness
Like the Moon and the Stars

Being near you is blissful
I'm a drunk in a bar,
Happy only at nighttime.
Like the Moon and the Stars

But our time is not ready,
Out patience slightly under par.
For that I will just stay loving you
My Moon and Stars.

# Perfection

When God made humans
He made us equal, but had one exception.
He created a woman equivalent to
Moon and stars, He made, perfection.

Her hair was brown as oak
And was silk to the touch.
Her presence undoubtedly known,
Though she never expected it much.

Her eyes brown as a doe
Yet captivating like the sea.
I grow yearning for her stare
Wishing for her muse to be me.

Her smile could part the ocean
Leaving all in silent awe.
Her lips are like venom
One small dose would do the job.

Her voice rings out like
A chorus of angels above.
Her tone can shake a mountain
Or be gentle like a dove.

To witness this perfection
One be considered blessed
To run fingers on her skin,
Even fewer can attest.

For she is a glimpse of heaven
Leaving all only wanting her more.
Loving this woman is easy,
But when she is gone, your heart will be torn.

If you get the mere chance,
I beg you to pay attention.
For I will always want that woman
The one God named, Perfection.

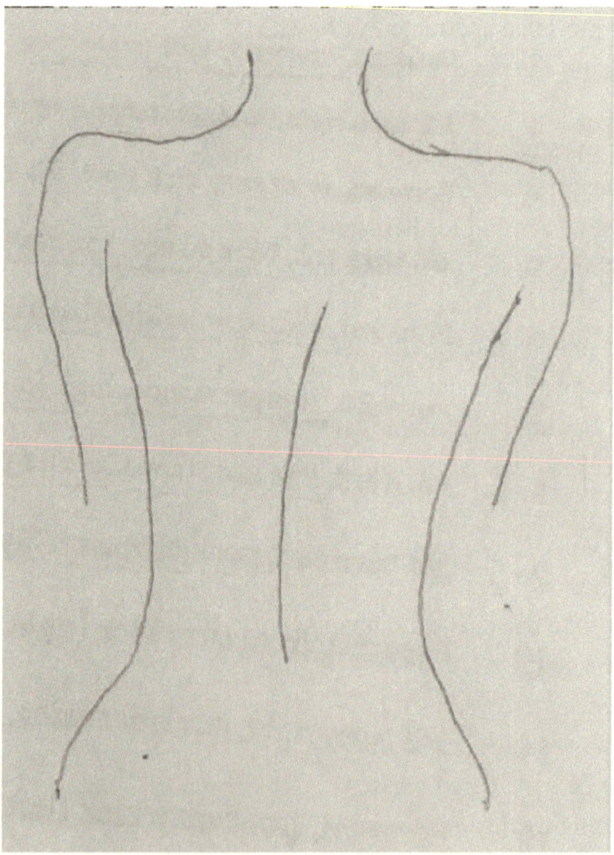

# Chapter 2. Losing Love

## Divorce.

The word is as vicious
As what follows after.
It brings nothing but clouds.
An extinction of laughter.

Questions of failure
And what could have been.
Creates a world of doubt
Stronger than any sin.

The heart feels empty
As the memories start to fade.
Was there ever any happiness
In the mess that was made?

It's not the closing of a chapter,
Rather the ending of a book.
Tears cover the pages
For all the time that it took.

It's hard to tread water,
Or ever stay on course.
The conclusion of that word.
That evil word. Divorce.

# Never Change

You correct your mistakes
Like a teacher grading a test.
You become the best version of yourself
In hopes you are still wanted.
But your hopes of a better you
Still fall short.
You are crushed and devastated.
The best version was still not enough.
The metamorphosis of what you became.
Was a mere product
Of what you thought they wanted.
Stay the worm you knew to be.
Don't change into the butterfly
That you know nothing of.

## The Ironic Curse.

The situation comes rare,
But when it does, its known.
The sadness and grief
Causes the mighty to atone.

It's like the hungry
Choking on scraps.
The hunter falling to demise
From one of his own traps.

The swimmer drowning.
The flyer descending.
The reader going blind.
The sturdy starts bending.

The small lies to spare
the slightest sorrow.
Are all still known,
And carry through tomorrow.

This feeling of happiness
Comes paired with gloom.
It's from knowing your feelings weren't
My doing to cause bloom.

But the small victory is cheerful
And for that I am traversed.
I am now trapped in this situation.
This Ironic Curse.

# Finding Strength

You fake a smile
Just to avoid the worry.
But behind closed doors,
All the despair makes everything blurry.

Getting dressed becomes a task.
The darkness is harder to ignore.
When will happiness return?
Why can't you feel adored?

And that is what this monster does.
This beast we labeled depression.
It breaks you down on your knees.
It's an unlearnable lesson.

It's something that's eternal.
Do not underestimate its length.
The beast will always crave you.
As you continue Finding Strength.

## Breaking Up with Yourself.

When you end a relationship,
You aren't just leaving someone.
You are bidding farewell to a part of yourself
And the things you have done.

The way you carried yourself
And the mannerisms that were made.
Now feel like a curse when committed.
Even if you wish they could stay.

The way you laughed,
The way you cried.
The way you wanted to love someone,
But, always felt denied.

Like your relationship you need to let it go.
That part of you is gone like the love it created.
It's too painful to look back and think on it.
Leaving you wanting to be sedated.

So, do to your old self like the notes and pictures.
Crinkle them up and set them on a shelf.
Keep yourself from any further pain.
Finish Breaking Up with Yourself.

# Final

One final thought,
One final feeling.
To express my love,
While my heart begins peeling.

Stay strong, stay focused.
But above all, stay true.
Keep smiling and laughing.
Never allow your days turn blue.

A blessing and an angel.
One of a kind is still one too many.
When anyone needs some extra love
You always happen to have plenty.

As my moon goes away,
My muse goes into hiding.
Forever know the love you kindled
Will stay strong and guiding.

My final thought,
My final feeling.
When you find your sugar high
Always stand with him, never start kneeling.

# Stronger

You thought this part of
Your life would be the best.
The future seemed only bright.
No fears of the dark.
Words and reassurance keep you
from needing a lifeline.
How was it that things fell apart?
How could they have quit on you?
You thought you could make it
through thick and thin.
You thought they would have
fought like you did for so long.
You thought they were stronger.
But you were wrong.

# Not Who I Thought

Once you brought me joy
You made me feel whole.
You provided me with comfort.
I felt we shared a soul.

I made mistakes.
I'm only human I must admit.
But the pain you brought on
Was torture not punishment.

I guess in the end
I can say I tried.
Even through the hard times
It wasn't my love that died.

But when I found out your truths
Weren't what you taught.
I can say deep down,
You were not who I thought.

# Lies.

Like a child playing in mud,
I found that with truth, you can mold.
The flexibility of my words.
How a weak lie can become bold.

It became an addiction.
The false truths made it easy.
The venom pouring out of my mouth
Would in time make me queasy.

My lies were long lasting.
Karma not quick, but it was strong.
I was met with consequences
That were fit for everything I did wrong.

Till this day I will hold onto the lesson
And cherish it until I die.
It's better to tell the truth
Then be haunted by a single lie.

# Tarnished Armor

You grew up hearing stories
Of a knight in shining armor.
He saved his princess from danger.
Nothing was able to harm her.

And when you became older
You found what you thought was a knight.
He sang to you and escorted you around.
Each day with him felt right.

But as time progressed
That feeling of love became faded.
Songs no longer sang.
Your love started to become jaded.

Your fairy tale ending was put on hold.
The knight was nothing but a charmer.
Unfortunately, it's hard to see the truth,
He was always wearing tarnished armor.

# Left Wanting.

Was it the words I said?
Was it the actions completed?
Is that what caused the hurt?
Making our love depleted?

Moving on wasn't an option.
You said you'd never find another.
But two weeks passed
And you are calling someone else lover.

So, you outgrew me.
Your new life is nothing but taunting.
As I sit and wait.
Finding myself, left wanting.

## Greater Than Memories

That kind of crazy,
Where one can't fall asleep.
They lie awake and ponder
While the memories start to creep.

You check your snaps
And type out a text
Just to delete it.
Questioning what to do next?

The pain in hindsight.
Knowing what could have been,
Engulfs you in an ocean
You feel as if you sinned.

Looking to the future
Trying to leave the past alone.
Is the hardest thing to accomplish,
Time is the only healer known.

Smile and put on the act.
Let them know you are fine.
Your chances blow away in the dust
As you walk that lonely thin line.

Though they are not yours
Remember them like a cool breeze.
For in your mind, this love of yours
Is greater than memories

# Broken Shell

Losing love is a lot like going to the beach,
Wading through water as it starts to swell.
Wanting to be a part of that scene of beauty.
Only to be seen as a Broken Shell.

You watch others flock on the shoreline.
Finding perfect shells to take home.
As you are left stranded in the sand.
Defects covered by the sea foam.

Once you were like those other shells.
Beautiful; carried like a token.
Then you were discarded by your person.
And as they left, you became broken.

Now you spend your days sitting in the sun.
Wishing to be picked up and cherished.
Wanting to only be special again.
Before the thought of love has perished.

# Nothing to You.

I tried replacing all the memories
With any possible outlet.
I traveled, read, talked and cried.
But I haven't found the answer yet.

Why is your face all I see
when I lay down at night?
Why do I crave your attention
when it only leads to a fight?

I plead to any higher power
To mute your voice from my ears.
I drink till I can't feel.
But I can never stop these tears.

Spending endless time searching
For anything or anyone old or new.
But in the end of it all,
They hold Nothing to You.

# Small Light

My life was consumed.
Grim, sad, and filled with dark.
My future seemed bleak.
No adventure to embark.

Then as I fell,
I caught a small sight.
I found my solace.
I saw that small light.

My strength returned.
My sadness departed.
I began to smile.
Oh, what has that light started?

I finally reached out
I felt the light
It was touching heaven
I held it so tight.

But the light was too bright.
I loosened my grip.
As the light soared high.
I felt my world begin to slip.

I may never keep that star.
But, oh I just might.
Forever find happiness.
Loving that small light.

# Special Spot

It could be a room,
A church, parking lot, or car.
That place that made you feel safe,
Even when everyone else was afar.

Sometimes you would have company.
And sharing the spot felt so great.
The memories you all created,
All of love and none of hate.

And time continued to pass,
The others stopped meeting.
You were again alone in your spot.
And those memories began retreating.

But you hold on to hope.
You do what the others could not.
You keep showing up and waiting
To have company at your Special Spot.

## Rear View Mirror

Life is a lot like driving a car.
A brand-new model with no miles.
Overtime the paint will chip.
Rust appears from all its trials.

And just like a curse,
How I wish I'd see clearer.
To never get trapped,
Staring through that rear view mirror.

All the miles traveled,
The trips life provided.
All the passengers that accompanied,
Now just relationships divided.

I'm told the objects in the mirror
Are closer than they appear.
Now the passenger seat is empty,
And the wheel becomes hard to steer.

Still stuck in that mirror,
My car crashes and breaks down.
I'm left on the side of the road.
With no other headlights around.

# No Air.

It was like a punch in the gut.
I couldn't believe it was true.
You were taken away from me.
I was left without a clue.

You should still be here.
We still had so much time.
A world without you in it,
Is nothing short of the greatest crime.

Why couldn't it be me instead?
You come back and I will leave.
You were loved by so many,
If it were me there'd be less to grieve.

With you no longer in my life,
I tend to just sit and stare.
I only wish to breathe you again.
But I am left with No Air.

# My Worst Enemy

I always wondered how it could be.
To be a superhero, my own super me.
What could stop me, or make me break?
What foe would test me, what would it take?

Then I grew up, and I felt like that hero.
Had all I worked for, never felt like a zero.
I soon had doubts, my fights closer to home.
There were no more bad guys, I was alone.

For it wasn't a man or woman, young or old.
It wasn't the smartest or strongest, I'm told.
The real fight was there, I just couldn't see.
The despair and sadness began to engulf me.

I make the lies, tell others not to worry.
To stop the concern for what is hurting.
My emotions start to lose full control.
My anger and sadness take its final toll.

Dimness is now what was once bright.
Normality is my new brand; I lost all fight.
Alone in the dark, I can finally see.
It's always been me. My own worst enemy.

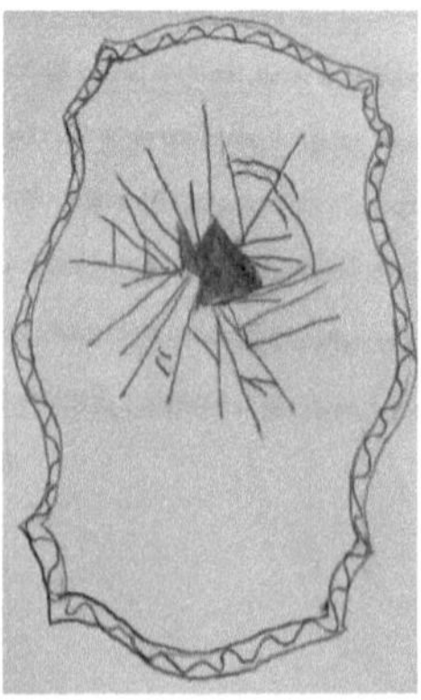

# Chapter 3. Everything Awesome After.

## Above the Peaks.B

When I was young,
I would stare at the sky.
I'd wonder how high it was.
And ask the question, "why?"

Why was this ocean
Unable to be reached?
Then one day I saw the mountains.
I longed to climb above the peaks.

Could a little child like me,
Make it through the rough terrain?
Or would I falter
And let the wind take my remains?

My hands will blister.
My body bruised and bloody.
My hair disheveled.
My face worn and muddy.

But what if I made it,
If I conquered that beast?
Would there be a celebration?
Would I feel honored at the least?

As the climb continued,
The years made me wise.
It wasn't about touching the sky.
It's not all about its size.

The journey I have sought out.
The trials I have beat.
Was the true victory,
That brought me to my feet.

I may not ever touch that sky.
Or find what all others seek.
But my success through failing
Is what put me, Above the Peaks.

# Hey Stupid.

Life is an ever-changing obstacle course.
You will trip, stumble, and even fall.
But you will get back up.
You might fail on that course.
You might need to step back and reevaluate.
You might need a break and walk away.
Just keep trying.
As long as you keep standing back up.
You will pass that course.
And when you find yourself standing on that podium of champions.
Remember it was you who got you there.
Relish it. Embrace it. Accept it.

# Mother's Baby

You gave me life.
You watched me grow.
You have seen me at my high.
You pulled me up from my low.

No matter what decisions I made.
I always had you at my side.
Whether good or bad,
You were there with great stride.

No matter what life threw,
You would face it with a shrug.
Even at my worst moments,
You healed with just a hug.

So, when life gets hard,
And I feel I'm going crazy.
Know I get solace,
In being my Mother's baby.

# My Old Man

You held me up
When I was born.
You held me close
When my heart was torn.

You let me lose,
When I needed to fall.
But you held me high
When I needed to feel tall.

You taught me life
And how to live.
You gave me all
Your love to give.

You raised good men
As yours did for you.
You mirror all his greatness,
That much is true.

Now that I'm older,
It's clear you had a plan.
My father, my pops, my dad.
My Old Man.

# God's Grace

Days are nothing but mystery.
Nights filled with terror.
The country is divided.
Fault shows no bearer.

During this time,
I fell so deep.
I drank away the days.
I had nights with no sleep.

But then I fell to my knees.
I called out your name.
Suddenly I was at ease.
The wild was now tame.

You washed away my despair,
And filled me with hope.
I began to see clear,
As I climbed that steep slope.

I can see my purpose.
My path no longer a maze.
And it is all thanks,
To our God's Grace.

# Friends

When times got too dark,
And family was never enough.
I'd feel weak and pathetic.
Each day felt more and more rough.

And without even asking
One or all would appear.
Like a small miracle,
I was protected from any fear.

My friends always found a way.
They'd take my problems as their own.
They'd accompany me on a dismal journey.
They would reap the seeds I have sown.

Whether a phone call or a hug,
My friends were there through it all.
I was always planted back on my feet,
Every time I would stumble and fall.

When my problems all die out
And they fade out like all the trends.
I know I will always have them.
Forever blessed with my Friends.

# Cat Daddy

Waking up in a foreign country
Always brought me anxiety.
Hearing the helicopters overhead
With no sign of tranquility.

Then one warm day
While sitting on the ground.
I heard a faint meow
And my heart grew with the sound.

You were cautious yet curious.
I knew you only wanted food.
So, I offered what I could.
I think we both understood.

You were an animal
Just trying to eat.
I was an animal,
Who wanted my heart to feel a beat.

As the days continued
You grew trusting.
I almost touched you.
At the seams I was busting.

When I was at my low
You let me touch your fur.
I cried the first night
When you let out a purr.

I will never forget that tour
And I won't forget you Matty.
Thanks for being my first fur baby.
It was an honor being your Cat Daddy.

# Fuzzy Zoloft

You entered my life,
When I didn't know I needed you.
You were just meant to be a pet.
A companion on my travels.
But, when I lost it all,
You stayed closer to me than anyone.
You cuddled me when I was alone.
You dried my cheeks when they
were flooded by tears.
Your tiny bark kept the demons away.
Your paws kept that barrel concealed.
You devoted every day to
fetching my happiness.
As soon as I lost it,
You quickly brought it back.
No medication could cure me.
But you saved me.

# Feel the Rain

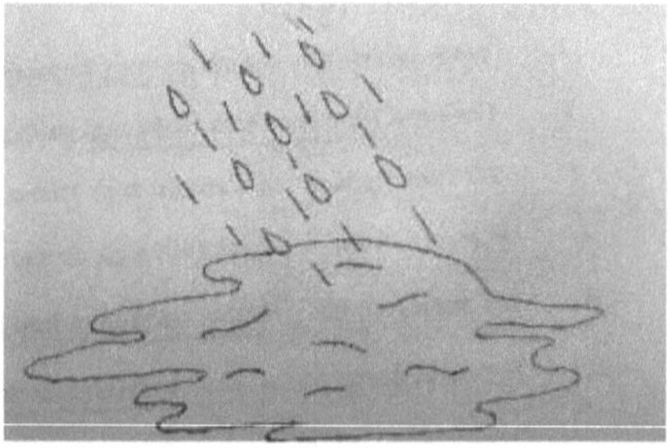

Life is hard,
It hits with ferocity
and breaks down even
the strongest warriors.
In my times of grief
I find myself not longing
For the sun.
I crave to feel the rain.
Having the water drops
Wash over me and comfort,
Like a blanket knitted from
A grandmother.
I am centered in a storm.
The rain and I become one.
My heart beats in sync
With the drops hitting my skin.
As the water falls to the ground
My worries and sadness follow.
I become an empty slate
Ready to rebuild.
So, bring me the downpours.
Bring me the monsoons.
My happiness will shine
Like a sun in the storm.

# Last, First Christmas

No one knew it then,
When they wished you a Merry Christmas.
But it was the last one you'd spend on earth.
Now warm weather isn't the only one missed.

The cheers and laughter
Seem lack luster from before.
The emptiness with you gone,
Becomes too hard to ignore.

The only solace in knowing you are gone.
Is the thought of all you have this year.
Surrounded by those who went before you.
Picturing you smiling from ear to ear.

Reuniting with your love
And receiving the earful of a lifetime.
Taking the verbal lashing in stride.
Getting there late was your only crime.

I only ask when you look down from above,
Is to know you are so loved and missed.
But all in all, I hope you enjoy in heaven,
Your Last, First Christmas.

## Without Capes

We awake in the morning,
Some of us late afternoon.
Most are accustomed to daylight
Yet some only see the moon.

We work like everyone else,
But sometimes we face trials.
These dangers can take their toll
Leaving a stare reaching up to miles.

We are hated, sworn at, and sometimes
We find ourselves under attack.
But if we get the call to help others,
Our drive to save will never lack.

We see birth and death.
The bad always outweighing the good.
But we come to work every day,
And carry ourselves like we should.

We act like a superhero
Only we can feel the pain.
The bumps and the bruises,
Physically and mentally, we begin to drain.

We never quit though
For we swore to serve and protect
So, I beg you this one time,
To spare a little respect.

We might not have superpowers
And some of us might be out of shape.
But we continue to protect and love.
Just like super heroes without the cape.

# My Home Jersey

My home Jersey isn't worn in sports.
It's not to be hung in halls.
It doesn't live on cereal boxes.
It's not worn by children in malls.

My Home Jersey is Blue.
With logos on the side.
Stitches and creases,
Easily worn against the tide.

My Home Jersey is complete,
With a shiny shield on the chest.
The only special identifier,
To tell me from the rest.

My Home Jersey isn't favored.
It hears more boos than Dallas.
Responding with it to save others,
I am still met with all the malice.

Every day I wear my Home Jersey.
I wear it with honor and pride.
I wear it to remember those who wore it
And no longer stand by my side.

When I remove my Home Jersey
The feelings stay intact.
I will never choose another Jersey
And that is a guaranteed fact.

## Lose the Love, Embrace the Hate

I spent my life wanting to
Be liked by everyone,
Now my job requires me,
To be hated till the shift is done

Once greeted with hellos
And a smiling face.
To now being flipped off
And called a huge disgrace.

I rarely get a thank you.
It's mostly just disdain.
I am viewed as a heartless robot,
Unable to feel pain.

Protect and serve
Try to not nibble at the bait,
Or else you will add to the fire
With an alarmingly scorching rate.

But I press on, as all officers do
To keep their community safe.
We keep helping, saving, and giving
Just as the ones before us gave.

As time presses on
And the day is getting late.
Do as you always have done,
Lose the love, Embrace the Hate.

## Be the Soap

We roll with the punches
That never seem to end.
We get looks and are hated,
When we only want to be a friend.

We deal with thieves, liars,
And some who sling dope.
But when times get hard,
I become the soap.

Yes, the item that makes
us smell clean,
Is the item that posses
something that is unseen.

For the ballad of this item
We call soap on a rope,
Is a story we all possess,
And that story is hope.

No matter the pressure,
Water or man.
We stay resilient,
Doing the job as we can.

Somedays we get worn.
Somedays we might slip.
But at the end if it all,
We always finish the trip.

So, when the day is long
And I find myself losing hope.
I have a small laugh and tell myself,
Be the Soap.

## Conversation with the Clouds.

From staring at their shapes,
Wondering what animal it was.
I found myself fascinated,
With the clouds above.

They'd block out the sun,
When my eyes were blinded.
They would carry heavy downpours.
But I never really minded.

Then one day you were taken from me.
And my heart became chrome.
For I knew the bringers of rain,
Were now what you called home.

At first, I was broken.
I felt completely lost.
Just to hear you call my name,
I would pay any cost.

Then I realized the beauty of it all.
You never really went away.
As long as I had the clouds,
Your spirit was here to stay.

So, I'd sit and stare above.
Speaking quietly and sometimes loud.
Feeling like you were right beside me.
Having a conversation with the clouds.

# Beating Rock Bottom

So much time was spent there,
That it became a temporary home.
The darkness and the gloom
Made sure that you'd never be alone.

Through all that time,
You decided that it would be no more.
No longer would you go through life
And have it feel like it was a chore.

Dig down deep and grit your teeth.
The climb wouldn't be easy or short.
But the realization of a brighter horizon
Provided winds for your ship to leave port.

The pain and anger slowly shed.
Your smile finally returns.
That spark ignites that fire,
And oh, how beautiful it burns.

Leaving sins in the past.
Destroyed like Gomorrah and Sodom.
You can look down and smile
At the feeling of Beating Rock Bottom.

# It Only Gets Worse from Here.

The wisest words came from an old man.
He made sure his statement was clear.
He looked me in the eyes and told me.
"It Only Gets Worse from Here."

His words left me confused.
How could his advice sound so bleak?
How were these words of encouragement?
The strength I sought appeared so meek.

He smiled as he saw my expression.
He said, "I know you are now a man.
But as you grow older with life,
Someday you will understand."

And just as that man predicted,
The word's meaning became deeper.
And though that man had passed.
That sentence was now a keeper.

It wasn't about things getting worse.
The meaning was pure bliss.
Taking this long to understand,
So foolish that it was missed.

"It only gets worse from here"
Meant that you had that best day.
One unforgettable moment
That no other moment could take away.

The birth of a child, getting that job,
Or maybe it was finding the love of your life.
No matter what moment,
It always held you up during any strife.

There would still be good times
As you traveled along the way.
But nothing close to comparison,
At the top that moment would stay.

So, every morning good or bad
When I'm standing in the mirror.
I have a laugh and I tell myself,
"It Only Gets Worse from Here."

www.ingramcontent.com/pod-product-compliance
Lightning Source LLC
Chambersburg PA
CBHW050025170726
48282CB00025B/546
* 9 7 8 8 1 8 2 5 3 8 9 6 2 *